ME AND GOD

A Book That Force You To Take A Look

Taimoor Ajmal

ISBN: 9798402746718
ASIN: B09QJ4KY5M

With gratitude to my friends and family, whose unwavering support made this journey possible. Special thanks to my mentor, Sonia Fernanda, for her invaluable support.

CONTENTS

INTRODUCTION

"Me and God," by Taimoor Ajmal, is a thought-provoking novel that embarks on a journey exploring the realms of spirituality, self-discovery, and the intricate interplay of political and social dynamics. Set against the backdrop of diverse landscapes and cultures, the narrative weaves a tapestry of philosophical reflections, mystical encounters, and the relentless pursuit of the divine. Through the lives of compelling characters like Sikandar, Rajwan, Saad, and Saleema, the novel invites readers to question their own beliefs, navigate the complexities of the self (nafs), and confront the challenges posed by external forces. Tackling issues ranging from the individual's quest for God to the manipulation of political systems, the story unfolds with a blend of mystery, spiritual insight, and socio-political intrigue. "Me and God" not only explores the intellectual and spiritual dimensions but also holds a mirror to societal structures, fostering a global dialogue on themes of unity, tolerance, and the universal search for purpose. With its potential to impact readers emotionally, intellectually, and spiritually, the novel transcends borders to contribute to a broader literary and cultural conversation.

Me And God

A Book That Force You To Take A Look

Author: Taimoor Ajmal

PREFERENCE

What inspires a person to conquer mountains despite their limitations? What compels someone to confront a storm headfirst? And how do some individuals evolve from being timid mice to fearless lions, while others become timid and apprehensive? They are ideas.

In our world, ideas are everything. They have allowed humanity to achieve remarkable feats, but they have also led us to do things worse than animals. Ideologies shape our emotions, character, beliefs, and hopes. Without ideas, we would not be truly human. Every individual has their own unique idea that drives them forward. Ideas are the birthplace of feelings, emotions, beliefs, and questions.

However, these same things can also weaken ideas. When a new and opposing idea clashes with your own, it can create a complex web of change. The first line of defense for your beliefs is often attacked, and the strongest weapon used in this assault is questioning. Over time, this questioning can gradually overwhelm you.

It's unfortunate that when ignorant ideas perish, it can be seen as progress for humanity, but when superior ideas are lost, it's a disservice to us all. Let's take a look at these two theories. The first one posits the existence of God, while the second one argues that God does not exist.

Upon closer examination, these two theories possess the power to challenge our fundamental understanding of human thought. The notion of a superior force, one that transcends any specific religion, can endow an individual with the capability to perform miraculous acts that others may find impossible. This force's belief provides solace and hope, enabling individuals to navigate even the most arduous of circumstances.

Taking the time to step outside of your own world can be a valuable lesson in empathy and understanding. When faced with the temptation to harm someone unjustly, it's important to remember that there may be consequences beyond what we can see. It's comforting to know that there is a higher power watching over us, and that justice will eventually be served. When faced with a difficult situation, holding onto this hope can provide the strength and guidance needed to persevere.

If you want to experience a sense of power and confidence, imagine that your close friend is the prime minister or army chief of your country. This will give you a newfound sense of courage and strength to stand up against your enemies. Additionally, knowing that your friend holds significant sway over the country can provide a feeling of security in times of financial hardship, as you can expect their support. Ultimately, it's all about having belief and awareness of the power structures at play in your life.

Just try to picture a mighty force that governs every single aspect of our world, from the tiniest particles to the grandest wonders. Believe in this divine power with unwavering faith, and be prepared to encounter awe-inspiring beings of immense strength and capability that you never thought possible. With this unshakable belief in the omnipotent force that guides us, you will feel empowered to face any challenge that comes your way.

When doubts about God's existence arise, fear will quickly take over, robbing one of the courage necessary to confront any challenge. This fear will imprison them, preventing them from living life to the fullest.

Without an ultimate judgment or higher power to govern your actions, you may fall prey to a materialistic mindset. You might believe that sin and reward are irrelevant, and only seek goodness that directly benefits you. However, sin only results in loss.

You may become so independent that even animals might find you shameless at times. It's possible that you possess a small amount of power if you can move mountains from their place. As a responsible individual, prioritizing the safety of others should be at the forefront of even the smallest actions.

Acting as your own protector and remaining vigilant is imperative as miracles are not always guaranteed. Have you ever delved into philosophical and metaphysical questions about God? This novel features an array of stories from individuals of diverse backgrounds who explore these inquiries in depth.

The novel Me and God is an enthralling read, that transports readers into a world full of enchantment and exploration. Starting from a modest abode in a small village, the story takes you on an incredible journey that leads to a magnificent palace and beyond.

Along the way, you'll encounter a wide range of emotions such as love, passion, insanity, serenity, and rebellion, all of which will ignite a spark within you to take action. The book is divided into five distinctive scenes, each more exhilarating than the last. Prepare to get lost in this captivating tale!

In the course of the narrative, the protagonist in every scene faces a plethora of situations, conditions, and setbacks, all of which are affected by a range of factors that shape their choices. However, their ultimate objective remains steadfast. Every hero traverses a distinct route to reach their destination, confronting their uncertainties with rational justifications and evidence.

I have observed that the profound comprehension and instructions of our religion are frequently confined to scholars and not readily available to the masses. Likewise, the teachings of love and its enigmas are often solely imparted to the youth. Consequently, I have taken the initiative to unite these two facets and make them more easily accessible to all.

Upon conducting extensive research, I discovered a significant gap in Urdu literature that lacked exploration of atheism. This sparked my determination to embark on the challenging task of composing a short novel with a neutral stance on religion, centered around this theme.

The process was demanding, requiring countless hours dedicated to perfecting each sentence. However, I am delighted to announce that my novel has proven to be a compelling and relevant tool for both Muslims and believers, empowering them to combat irreligion and stand up for their faith with conviction.

Not only has the novel been translated into Spanish, but it is also currently undergoing translation in various other international languages besides Urdu and English. I cannot express enough gratitude to all those who have supported me throughout this journey, with a special thanks to Jitendra Sahib for his unwavering efforts in ensuring the publication of the novel again, and in an even better condition.

Throughout this book, the research of Dr. Zakir Naik has been utilized to explore the subject of comparative religions. Additionally, when introducing the self in certain chapters, guidance was taken from Muhammad Nasir Ifthar's book "From Self to God". As for chapters 10 and 11, which cover the topic of intelligence agency matters, insights were gleaned from Brig. (R) Syed Ahmad Irshad Tirmidhi, the former Chief of Staff who drew from the Directorate General of ISI's book "Sensitive Institutions".

This book is being translated into multiple languages for readers worldwide. Despite its concise length, it covers a comprehensive range of topics related to life and highlights all the crucial aspects. Anyone who reads it is sure to find something that resonates with them. Rest assured; this novel will have a positive impact on your life after reading it.

If I have made any errors, I sincerely hope that the readers will find it in their hearts to forgive me.

Supplicant: Taimoor Ajmal Awan

A LOGICAL REBELLION AGAINST GOD.

Suddenly darkness fell in front of my eyes. But the light returned as fast as if it had never gone back. After a little restoration, I realized that the bus in which I was riding had now been involved in an accident and at the same time I felt a slight tingling sensation, but the fire As soon as I heard the sound, there was a strange movement in my body and all the passengers who were trying to get out of the bus were probably blind who could only see themselves Maybe God was showing us a glimpse of the Doomsday or the punishment for sin but no there was also a good deed, then why the punishment (of sins) instead of Reward (for good deeds) But no, it was probably not a punishment for sin, nor was it a strong defense in goodness. until now, my life was spent in doubt about their existence (sins & goodness). But don't know why these were taking over my mind today? Perhaps this was the effect of the voices of passengers who were constantly calling to their God. But I also heard that what happens is by the will of God, so why were they calling on him Knowingly? He(God) probably did it all, did he just want to hear their cries or did he just want to make his presence felt? But why does he makes us realize his presence by giving us hardships? there may be other ways. It might be the driver's fault. But why it happened today? Why we were punished because of his fault? How we handed over our lives to him But he didn't force us to do it. We handed our Lives to him with our own will. But........ Suddenly there is an explosion voice raise. Then the eyes begin to close, feeling a strange calm.

The train is moving towards the destination at full speed, Moonlight

night with deep silence making it more attractive. Suddenly hearing someone's voice he came out from the world of imagination.

Brother! "Take care of your fallen mobile phone, otherwise someone will pick it up" and after saying this, he went to the front seat. He thanked him with a slight smile and later he kept looking at this person with excuses, maybe it was something strange in his getup. What bothered him was how could this man be so honest despite his strange appearance?

And then he went to the valleys of sleep thinking about that why Every God of the World give rewards only on Goodness Even though he has invented sin's(evil) when a servant (men) does evil why is the property of Iblis or Satan revealed to him? Does God's power weaken then? Or do they both have equal power? Sometimes God wines and sometimes Satan. Whoever wins owns it. Or are God and Satan two different names for the same being? Who has labeled various movements if you do something good then God is ruling over you and if you do something bad then satan is ruling over you or is it all just a game of human thinking?

He was very happy in his Heart sitting in these beautiful mountains that I have loved the God's creature, now I will receive the love of God But because of the sudden sound of Gunfire and the raising pain in his body, he comes out of the world of these thoughts. This is the only sound he can hear after that: "Come on! Let's go, he will die, if anyone sees us, it will be a problem for us."

The voices were gone but now a scream had started inside him. He was asking the question to God that you were watching everything and I just wanted to reach you, to whom society called them your Saints(wali/Peer). They told me that the only way to reach God is through his creation.

Oh, God!!!! Isn't women your creation? I went to love creatures, you instilled the love of women in my heart, you are the controller of heart or not? You know that my love is pure, maybe you don't even know it? You are Even closer to the aorta or is it just a consolation given by a wise man to give hope to the weak? If you knew, why would all this happen? Maybe you have chosen some servants (men) whom you only want to love from them to their race? Why did you make this distinction? Rather, your demand from us human beings is for justice and equality.

He was very careful with his gun slung over his shoulder. Suddenly he felt a commotion in the bushes in front of him and he fired a shot and a voice came from the front "O God!!".

The soldier again fired and now from the front, there was complete and deep silence.

He was also ready to pile the enemy again. But after that, he went to a deep thought that why should it fight behind/for the religion?

I remembered God when I shot the bullet. Whom I shot he Also remembered God. But maybe God likes my religion that's why God has not saved him on his call or maybe we both were in the wrong religion, God was with someone else's religion. Therefore God leaves this decision based on "who has power will rule". But why doesn't God come forward (in front of the world) and sort out this matter or he likes this massacre? If a person of One religion dies at the hands of a person of another religion, his fellow religionists call him a martyr and non- religionists call him a hellish person. Either the dead of all religions are Martyrs or all of them are hellish or is human just doing all this in his stupidity or by using the name of God, the wise men using all humanity to achieve their goals for centuries. And its mind-building continues for a sacred religious purpose and who becomes a wise and raise question on this holy religious goal is killed, as they declared him infidel(kafir). Maybe this is the world of infidels. Here, a believer of one religion says infidel to the believer of another religion. And the believer of other religion says infidel to others religion person. Even the circle of infidels goes on and on like this world which is rotating in a circle.

Suddenly firing starts from cross-border and he engages in response to the firing.

He embraced the chieftain (Sardar) of the tribe and he was continuously crying.

The chieftain was repeatedly saying to him the same thing that "son revenge is

our right". Once we are done with the burial we will take our revenge.

He came back home after burying his father and two young brothers. Today he was full of displaced. Because his half-family had already died in a bomb blast. And the left one was killed by the soldier of the state Army today. It was just told by the chieftain that they were killed while fighting for their rights. The right which God gave them. And their religious fellows took their right from them.

Suddenly he screams while thinking about that whole Matter which happened to him.

Oooo, God!!!!!! Why this deception ?????

On one hand, you said the fight for your right, and on the other hand, if we fight for our right. They declare us Rebel and then kill us using your (God) religion references.

There is no existence of God. Now I understand the game of a wise man which he played to save his empire. Yes, I understand everything that why he(wise men) gave the concept of doomsday. So that the oppressed never become powerful by rebelling. Everyone just gives this hope to people like us that God will give Justice in the Hour(doomsday).

Now he had a strange smile on his face. In which the tears of the dead were hidden but they were very dim. His smile was stronger as he has known all the secrets of the universe.

THE REVOLUTIONARY WISDOM

When he opened his eyes, he found himself in a hospital, he was looking at the nurse standing nearby with questioning eyes.

The nurse spoke up before he could speak,

' you are slightly hurt, which caused you to faint.'

He asked a nurse ' What about that explosion and what happened to those passengers?

The nurse smiled slightly and spoke 'nothing can hurt you if God wanna keep you safe. The sound of the explosion you heard is the sound of the wheels of that bus that exploded.

He asked, 'What about a fire which I saw and those passengers who were shouting?

Nurse: if I were there I would make a video of you after you fainted so that I can answer all your questions but unfortunately I was not there and all passengers are safe with God's help.'

"God"! When he heard this word, he was shocked again!.

"It means God heard their prayers, it means God exists, Goodness prevailed, Sins were not punished. But how do I prove God?'

After speaking for a while, he spoke in his heart. If there is a God, then he must have created that intellect to prove his existence.

But where to find that person? Who can answer my questions without cursing me?

O, God! Show me the light, Reluctantly, he cried out to God.

After being discharged from the hospital, he now set out in search of God. He doesn't know where to find God. These questions were not new to him. He had asked these questions to the scholars of All religions. But in return, he was warned to lose his faith that not to think about such questions. With the help of religious references, they tried to provide him satisfaction but his demand was always rational.

So at last he thought of addressing himself, but what answers will he get from himself? If he has answers to his questions then why do the questions arise?

Now he was feeling helpless, so to kill himself, he picked up a knife from the table.

Suddenly an idea came to his mind and he stopped.

Who made this knife? It did not come into existence without a creator.

Now he was looking around. He saw the existence of different creators in everything. Some creators were hidden and some were obvious.

"Wow, God, wow," maybe you knew that man would question your existence. That's why you gave him the power to create. You kept answers to human questions inside himself. Yes, You(God) exist, but hidden, you can't be seen just like I can't see the creator of this knife. But that doesn't mean if I can't see the creator, there is no creator of the knife. The existence of a knife is testimony to the fact that there is a maker(Creator).

God! You're a reality and I wanted to prove you philosophically, while philosophy is a question, which stands up again with every answer, there is no destination for philosophy, it drives a person crazy. Now, if a man wants he can choose the answers that are the reality or choose the questions which are philosophy. The reality does not change, philosophy cannot change reality because questions can be changed, the reason is that there is no distinction between right and wrong in question. But if the answer is correct, it is satisfactory but if it is wrong we can correct it. The correct answer regarding God is that which is not witnessed by the human-made thing. Rather it is witnessed by the things which humans can't make or create. And they are witnessing that their creator does exist. Reality exists, and GOD is the reality. Just like the existence of a knife's creator is reality. Whether I can see the creator of this knife or not but I can't deny Its existence. . Not everything in this world came into being by itself. Not these tall buildings, not this mobile which is in my hand, not this internet signal. Although I can't see these signals. But I acknowledged their reality. God! When I can believe in the existence of unseen signals. So I believe in you too.

But God, who made you? Are you one or more than one? Do you have a son?

Dear, brother!

He suddenly came out of the valleys of his thoughts and replied, Yes.

What's bothering you that How can I be honest? Or is the difference in my appearance and action bothering you?

He replied, "don't mind but both".

The man with a strange appearance smiled slightly and replied, "Listen, young Boy! People measure things or actions by two things, on their own experiences or experiences (stories) heard from others. They are making mistakes because experiences are of the past and actions are of the present. As a result, the present forcefully has to become the same as the past and when the present is based on the experiences of the past, the same state becomes our future. That means, the past not only dominates the present, but it does not allow the future to come into being because the past becomes their base. Our present is always bound in the chains of the past, that is why our present never changes and When our present does not change, our future is not created. I'm not saying that experiences are useless. Rather, it is a very useful thing but only when human is Full of knowledge and consciousness. And able to think from every Angle, he should act smartly based on his experiences, but shouldn't take decisions. Rather, decisions must be free from the shackles of the past because every new action is different from the old one.

The form of every action may be the same, but the reason behind their being into existence or the consent behind doing it is different. Every time the intention is different. The day we start measuring things or actions from right or wrong angles, questions will arise not on personalities but Actions. It will bring peace and love. But remember, son, the actions which you have more will become your personality and society will decide what is your personality?

Now guess from here you found the actions and signs of beggars and thieves in me, that's why you quickly guessed my personality. The experience in your mind forced you to decide this. Now that you have guessed my personality but suddenly I acted against my personality. Because of which your mind raised questions about your experiences. Take a moment to move away from past experiences that are safe in your mind or forget the past. Your mind will immediately accept this new experience, that a person who looks like a thief and a beggar can also be honest. Do you know why this will happen? Because you defeated the past experiences that ruled in your mind. Two governments do not exist on one land at one time, there is always war that keeps on going continuously, A proper system cannot be built… If you want to maintain an organized system, so you have to form a single government, past or present. The government of the past is a little riotous. But son, without it you can form the present government, but it will be weak, it will break again and again."

So what should I do sir? You are preventing me from keeping the government of the past and you are also warning me about the present Government.

Son! "You have to find a middle way, you have to establish the present government over the past government."

So, Sir! Won't there be a war because of this?

Son, " you didn't get my point that you have to give limited authority to the government of past and you have to make a law, that the decision will be made by the present government, but it will also take into account the advice of Past Government. It will also save the self-respect of the past government and you will be able to keep a balance and the same balance that you will keep in the government of the past and present that you have established on land which is your mind, this balance will bring progress which will become your future.

Look, son! "The future is like a businessman, it comes where there is peace.

He thought to himself, he seems to be an intellectual person, he can answer my all questions.

Sir! He addressed the strange-looking man.

Yes, son!

Sir! What is your name?

When he opened his eyes, he found himself in a rotten room. When he felt a slight tingling sensation of pain, he screamed in pain.

Suddenly a weak but confident female voice echoed.

Son! " Be calm, there is no danger but the wounds are not so strong so carefully move. I stopped bleeding very hardly. I can't stop it if it starts again.

The young man said," who are you and what's your name?

Son, you will find out later who I am but my name is saleema. And what's your name son?

Saleema khatun(respected lady) my name is Ammar. How did I come here saleema khatun? And why do you live here alone in the middle of these mountains?

Saleema: Son! I was grazing goats, as usual, I found you, your blood was flowing, I thought of helping you and I brought you here.

Ammar: But khatun, how did you bandage my wounds?

Saleema: Hahaha my son! Before becoming anonymous in these anonymous valleys, I was a doctor. The bullets only touched you so I didn't have much trouble treating you.

Ammar: But khatun, how are you here?

Saleema: leave me, Ammar, how are you here?

Ammar: I went in search of God, someone said that love of creature (mankind/ human) will take you to the God he didn't clarify whether the love of a man or the love of a woman will take me to the God.

Saleema: Well then your real search is God. Someone told me the same way, I went that way I fell in love with a man, he took advantage of my love, I could not go home or live in society, so I decided to continue my journey and came here.

Ammar: So did you find God?

Saleema: Yes! But there is still a long way to go. Now we both are passengers of the same destination, I'll take you towards my position first then we will go for the remaining journey together.

Ammar: But what about love I had for God's creature? Do I have to give up?

Saleema: You have to be patient and have some courage as well. You will find the answers to every question.

He returned to his camp after completing his duty, where he had other soldier colleagues, he thought to ask them these questions but as soon he addressed his colleagues, everyone started congratulating him before he could say anything. He was a little surprised. But his colleagues handed him a letter from high officials (Military upper command Authority). What is this? He addressed everyone.

A colleague of his said, " Yasir congrats, I think you have got an honorary rank. Brother, we have not opened it. You open it yourself.

When Yasir opened the letter, he found the address of a place and a fixed date. Where he had to reach.

Colleagues said what is written?

Yasir told everything.

A colleague said you seem to have been transferred, someone said something, then someone said something.

Suddenly a colleague spoke up, "today I understood why we are only told to obey orders and why is it forbidden to make a big decision on your own (individual). As you can see, not all of us get agree in one place, so we have to follow the thinking of one so that we can become powerful and we must choose the thinking that has the ideology.

Go! Yasir, be happy wherever you are.

Yasir was persuaded to ask the colleague his questions but his inner fear stopped him. And he pressed these questions to his chest and started his journey.

There are two powers in the world, one is right and the other is wrong. Until one of them is established, this world will continue to be a battlefield. If the right power prevails, then this world becomes hell for the wrong power and if the wrong power prevails, then this world becomes hell for the right power. That's why there is no paradise in the world. Because every human being has a different angle of measuring right and wrong. So God has already told us what is right and what is wrong so that we do not get entangled in this rational game.

He was now in Sardar's (hetman) room. Sardar was putting him into agitation by saying that son revenge is your right, Khalid doesn't back out.

After a while, some men enter the room, and Khalid was ordered to go out.

After the men left, Sardar called Khalid to his room and said look, Khalid, I didn't know when this matter started, these men used to came here even before me and used to take the people of our tribe with them, we were told that they were going to avenge your loved ones. I don't know why our loved ones are dying, what is their crime? But every time their dead Bodies came back, my heart burns with revenge because even those dead Bodies went to avenge their loved ones. Tomorrow they will take you too with them, then you too will avenge your loved ones. But Khalid, you must have to find the answers that why the state is our enemy? Why do they call the dead bodies of our beloved ones traitors? Although they are our religion fellows and our religion teaches us to fight for the right. But who is the real thief of our rights? I want you to measure everything on the scale of wisdom.

Khalid: Sure Sardar, I'll do it.

THE SECRET OF FOUNTAIN/ GOD & DEVIL ARE SAME?

May these were the questions that once answered, leaving no room for further questions. But finding answers to these questions was no easy task. He remembered his time when he believed in God, He believed in its existence. One day he suddenly read a post on Facebook which shock the foundation of his faith. Alas, his faith was so weak that a small question shock his faith, weakened his faith. He had only options, either accepting the religious arguments or invent rational arguments or there was a third way he didn't want to go at all, which was to be an atheist, Denying the existence of God. And which religious argument does he accept? Some acknowledge God to some extent, some to another. He was completely confused. He still remembers that when he asked these questions to his close friends and relatives, he was answered: "Sikander, shut up! Your intellect cannot reach God".

But he always explained to them that I do not want to convey my intellect to God, but I want to persuade God with my intellect.

Now Sikander was somewhat satisfied because he had accepted God with his intellect, had acknowledged his existence. But there were still some questions.

He just went outside to get some fresh air.

He was drinking tea at a hotel in the bazaar(market). Suddenly he heard gunshots outside, he got a little nervous but after a while firing stopped, he went out to assess the situation.

He saw two dead bodies lying on a road, who was shot dead.

He came back to the hotel and asked the innkeeper, " who are these peoples who have been killed?"

Innkeeper: one is a local politician who was sure to win this election.

Sikander: And the second?

Innkeeper: The second was a very rich person of this Area.

Sikander: who killed them?

Innkeeper: Sir, someone killed him(rich person) in the lure of power, and another was killed by his son in the lure of money, but nothing can be said for sure.

Sikander: God bless them.

Sikander had just come out of the hotel and was walking towards the park and was thinking about the whole incident. He sat down on a bench in the park and began to enjoy the surrounding scenery. Suddenly a thought comes to his mind, Are there ever any changes that came to the universe system? The sun is still the glory of the day and the moon is the life of the night, have still their existence. The wheel of time is moving, God is one, if there were two or more, there would be a power struggle between them. Each God makes his Creation and those creatures kept fighting among themselves, the creature of God who won, that God was called Powerful. God would have their worlds, they would have different creatures, and it is obvious that every God wants his creation to be the most visible.

If God had a son, he would have changed the system, bringing the sun out in the night instead of the day, but neither the system changed nor any separate creature was discovered. That means God has no son, then God has no father. And even if it is accepted that God has a Son or a father, then this is how a society of Gods comes into being. In the same way, God will be called a creature. And can a creature create another creature?. If I could, humans would be a God of thousands of creatures today, and when everyone was a God, the very idea of creation would disappear. And when the concept of creation ends, who will call God a God?

Don't get too confused, just try to understand in simple language. If you go deeper into the invention of anything, you will be satisfied with its owner, but not with the inventor, because when it comes to invention, the human intellect does not recognize anyone as the ultimate inventor. Let understand this from an example, this mobile that is in your hand, you are the owner of it but you did not invent it. Let's just talk about its screen, the mobile company made a mobile screen with some grains, but the question arises as to who made these grains?

Son: my name is Aqil.

And what is your name, Son?

Mr.Aqil, my name is saad.

Mr. Aqil, there are some questions, can I ask you?

Saad son must ask.

Mr. Aqil, " why Every God of the World give rewards only on Goodness Even though he has invented sin's(evil) when a servant (men) does evil why is the property of Iblis or Satan revealed to him? Does God's power weaken then? Or do they both have equal power? Sometimes God wines and sometimes Satan. Whoever wins owns it. Or are God and Satan two different names for the same being? Who has labeled various movements if you do something good then God is ruling over you and if you do something bad then satan is ruling over you or is it all just a game of human thinking?"

Son, the answers to these questions are very simple.

Saad: Then, Sir, give the answers to these questions.

Mr. Aqil laughs and says, "Then come I will answer your questions".

They both go to the train canteen and take tea and while drinking tea Mr.Aqil starts his talk.

" Is it a crime to travel by train?

Yes and also no,

Yes, it is a crime to travel without a ticket, and it is not a crime to travel with a ticket.

Now listen carefully son, what we both have in common is travel, but still, we cannot call it common because your journey is legal and my journey is illegal(I don't have a ticket).

Let's make it very simple with a small example, Look, God has created a way to do everything. he rewards the servant(human) for working in his way but if a servant acts against his way, he(servant) deserves to be punished, as I have explained to you by examples.

Both of these ways are made by God but one of them is legal and the other is illegal.

Son, you have considered the state of Pakistan as the state of God and considered the enemy state as the state of Satan(shaitan). Now when the crime rate in the state of God will increase, would you say that the servants of the state of shaitan are ruling over the state of God's servant?

Saad: Yes, I'll say that.

Aqil: Hahahahah! Son, I think you should call those traitors, who break the law of the state of God and work on the ideology of the state of shaitan in greed for money or greed for wealth, because of the bad work of these peoples we cannot say that the kingdom of shaitan has come because the state of God still exists.

You know the most beautiful thing is that God has given freedom to his creature but created two ways one is legal and the other is illegal, look at the greatness of God's freedom, that he has given us, the freedom to choose, either obeying God's constitution or betraying it, choosing a reward or punishment, God's constitution gives method and limits, which is to our advantage.

And betraying his constitution means that we adopt something against the method listed in God's constitution. However, the constitution also shows the way for that thing.

Son, the matter is very straightforward. The two paths have different names from which their destination is determined the destination of the path of evil is bad and the destination of the path of Good is good, in the same way, travelers on these paths will be called travelers of good or evil.

Saleema and Ammar were now sitting near a fountain.

Saleema, addressing Ammar, says,

"Can you see the water flowing from the fountain? when you drink it from the place where the fountain is flowing in the beginning, it will be very fresh and sweet but let me take you to another place."

Saleema takes Amar to a salt mountain and says,

"Look at this fountain water, it will enter into the salt mountain from here. Now drink water before the entry point".

Ammar: The water is very fresh and sweet.

Saleema: Let me show you something else.

Now Saleema was standing with Ammar at the place where the fountain water had crossed the mountain of salt.

Saleema: Now drink water, Ammar.

Ammar drinks water and replies, the water is now bitter.

Saleema: Now listen carefully, Ammar, the shape of the water has not changed, nor its condition, it looks like it was coming out of a fountain, but it has changed, you will know when you drink it.

So your today lesson was very simple. That you are now drinking water from a fountain on the earth, which has come through thousands of salt mountains because you have been drinking the same water from the beginning, do you think it is the real water, but now doubts have arisen in your heart. After all, where does this water coming from, and is this its real existence? or is it mixed?

So son, The search for God is the same as that. your brain which is a fountain and your thinking which is the fountain of water, are no longer in their original state. To find its true state, you have to go back from the mountains of salt. Only then you will be able to feel the reality of thoughts. And when you feel the real state, you have to change the direction of the water.

Look, you will divide yourself. one will remain on the earth, and the other will go back from the mountains of salt in search of reality when you stop fountain's water from going to the salt mountains and find a clean way to get it to the ground(earth) and real water reaches yourself which is on Earth. Then the journey in search of God will begin.

But son this is not easy to do, because when you change the direction of water, water will not reach your earthly being(self) and if it stays thirsty for a long time, it will die, and if that being(self) dies. You will die too.

So Son, first makes a clear path and then change the direction of the water. Remember, in this work don't be too early or too late.

Ammar was looking at Saleema's face in surprise, suddenly with saleema's voice, he came back to the world of Consciousness.

Saleema: Think again! you can still go if you want to, but if you start, there is no need to hurry and delay.

Now he was on his way, after 2 days and 1 night he reached his destination, where there was a small check post, he showed the letter at the check post, they told him to rest and then blindfolded him and taken him to a training center. upon arrival at the training center the blindfolded was removed before he could look around suddenly someone punched him in the face and after that, someone else kicked him.

He was lying on the ground in excruciating pain and that's all he heard in someone's laughing voice, "welcome to the value of The eagles". After that, he found himself in the day valleys of sleep.

As soon as Khalid's blindfold was removed, he found himself on a chair in a spacious and luxurious hall, where there were probably other people but because of the darkness, he could not see anyone. Suddenly a voice echoes, "welcome to all of you, you are about to become part of the best organization in the world right now, which worships the truth away from lies, which fights for its rights. You all will be trained by the best trainers in the next few days and you will be part of the great mission, now you can all go to your rooms, whoever is called should get up from his seat and go to his/her room".

After waiting for a long time his name is called, when he arrives in his room, he is amazed, such a magnificent and dignified room he had probably seen only in his thoughts till today.

THE DOOR & THE NEW WORLD

Everything is God's innovation, this is the answer on which we satisfy ourselves. But some people have some strange thoughts. They ask strange questions from themselves. okay, questions are good but every question has the answer. But the answer doesn't need to find in the same era in which the question arises. Maybe the answer finds immediately but it is empty from logic and evidence. This type of answer which is without any logic and evidence is not acceptable in Infront of a wise man.

Let's go back ten centuries from today, You ask me a question, "can man step on the moon? I say, "yes! Man steps on the moon". You ask, "how?" I say "I don't know, but man can step on the moon". You will ignore me or my answer by understanding me crazy.

Now tell me, the answer which I gave in the tenth century was wrong? No!, Just because he was not considered to be true because it didn't have any evidence and logic.

Today, my old answer is being considered true because it now consists of logic and evidence.

So it is very important to understand here, that only a few percent of the human brain works. So according to this, human wisdom is limited and how can a limited thing raise questions about something unlimited?

Who is infinite and unlimited? This universe says science.

Who is the creator of this infinite universe? "God".

Now you can figure out what you're going to question.

Let's not confuse you too much. Let's go back to God.

Now Sikander began to think about the answers he had found from his wisdom. now he was counting his answers on his fingers.

1. God is exist

2. God is one

3. God is neither the father of anyone nor the son of anyone.

The question that came to his mind now was, Can God be seen?

When a soldier hits an enemy he is rewarded, but when an enemy kills a soldier and if he is caught, he gets punished. See, both of them are killing each other, but one is getting a reward for killing and the other is getting punished for killing. One is legal and the other is illegal. Although both will be right according to their ideology, if everyone starts fighting on their ideology, then human beings on earth will end. So to stop this ideological war, it is necessary to go to the ideology of the power that has made us. Power is that Which will never be weak. Those who are weak are not powerful. Therefore, the definition of power is that Which remains forever, that is the real power, and the remaining one is God, then God is the real power. And as far as human wisdom is concerned, it is powerful, for sometimes he(wisdom) also bring his rule. But wisdom is still in God's control. Because the wisdom (mind) changes based on the situation. But the situation never changes based on wisdom. Because in this world there is countless wisdom, and every wisdom (mind) has had a different ideology. Everyone sees the situation in the same way(death, storm, etc, etc), the situation can not be changed with the help of wisdom, Only God can change the situation because he has only the power. when the power is in one hand so hassles cannot arise, the decision is unavoidable (ultimate).

But when the power is not in one hand, a strong and decisive decision does not come to exist, there is always a hassle and the system does not run in case of hassles (disagreement). But we can see with our eyes that every particle of this universe going through a systematic system.

Aqil: I hope I answered you. Maybe, my answer was not comprehensive and not short but it is clear, you just focus on that answers, so the next time when you reach the answer, you can finish the new questions in their birth time, which can arise after any answer. Look, son, don't nurture questions too long. Try to get an answer as soon as possible.

Saad: yes of course

Now the train had reached its final station. After meeting each other, Aqil and saad move towards their destinations. Saad was now very happy because he had found somewhat answers to his questions. But was that the destination of his questions? No, because how can the questions that arise on an infinite caste (God) be limited? Somewhere, that infinite caste (God) has been addressed to his servant.

But every religion in this world says that they have the true commandments of God.

Where to find God?

But no, maybe God can be sought. As soon as this comes to his mind, he started trying to find God in some of the world's most famous religions.

He was now on the way to his journey. He now needed a guider on this Journey.

Ammar: I don't understand that you are forbidding me to hurry and also to be late, although the delay is good and life is not reliable so hurry is good too.

Saleema: If you delay, you will die without seeking God and if you hurry, you will fall into the traps of satan.

It's getting dark now. Go and rest. We have to go on a journey again in the morning.

Ammar now went to his hut which was made of wood. He was constantly thinking about Saleema. Who is this woman? How could she live here alone? What will be the story of her? Who was the man who took advantage of the love of such a good woman? But despite being so wise, how could this woman be deceived? Ammar's mind was flooded with such questions. But he tried to reassure himself that he would ask these questions from saleema in the morning.

The next morning, Saleema took Ammar on a new Journey.

Saleema: Ammar, you must be hungry, so we hunt first, then I will teach you today's lesson.

Ammar: Sure, I have some questions about yourself, can I ask?

Saleema: hahaha! Ammar, you will confuse yourself. You first find the destination of this journey, you first visit this world and then enter the new world. If you go to two worlds at the same time, you will get confused and you will not find the destination.

Ammar: But the question is how can a world be?

Saleema: The question is the door to a world and the answer is the whole world, As long as you don't have an answer, you're out of the door. When you get the answer, it means you're in the door. It is human nature that whenever he enters the new world, he wants to see the smallest detail of it. This is where he gets caught up in the maze of curiosity. The one who has crossed over is called a wise person and the one who is trapped by this, peoples call him mad.

I know what questions you have about me, I will answer you, but I will not let you in from the door, I will come out and answer you.

Ammar: is that possible?

Saleema: yes, It is possible. Now don't ask any more questions, now I'll give you practical answers, some language answers (mouth answer) are not satisfactory.

Now that his eyes were open, this time he found himself in a closed room. He was completely tied to the ropes. There was a dim light in the room coming from a window. Suddenly a gas began to spread in the room and at the same time, a sound came from a speaker in the room, "Young man, You only have 10 minutes to save your life. The ropes tied to your hands are poisoned if you resist and your hands bleed then will poison enter your blood, you will die in only 3 minutes, and if you do not die, poisonous gas Will kill you in 10 minutes, and if you succeed from everywhere, you will not be able to reach the window and if you can reach the window, the poisonous snakes wrapped there will not let you out alive. But if you want, you can save (escape). You have to find the way by yourself".

He was so lost in the colors of this room that he forgets all about the questions he had asked and the mission (goal) explained by the cheif (Sardar).

Alas, how weak is the mission which goes out of the mind when it sees wealth or difficulty. In fact, that is not the goal. There is only a temporary state of insanity. Which man angrily declared the goal(mission). In fact, the goal is man remembers it, whether it is heaven or hell, happiness or sorrow, rise or fall, he does not forget it. Rather every step he takes, no matter which direction he takes, is only to achieve his goal.

The next morning, as instructed, he arrives in a room where many more people are present. Soon a person enters the room and addresses everyone, " Welcome to the world of intellectuals, here we will teach you what a human being is and what his freedom is. Three things will be discussed in our basic lesson.

1. Religion

2. Rituals and customs

3. Society

First, we will understand them and at the same time, we will understand how to use them as our power and how to weaken the next one. Because they are so important to our mission (goal)".

Khalid: and what is our mission?

____

THE TRICK OF A HUNTER

As soon as this question came, He asked himself, "Can I see the signal? Can I see Ghost? Can I see a thing standing 1000 km away? No, but why?"

To get the answer, he first tried to understand the structure of the human eye from science. He was reading an article in which he wrote:

"The resolution of the human eye is not 576 megapixels. The structure of the human eye differs from that of the camera, although the basic principles of making an image from light are used in both camera and eye. Modern digital cameras have image sensors that have millions of pixels and all the pixels are the same. In contrast, the eye does not have pixels, but rather light-detecting cells of different types. Taken together, the human eye has about 120 million cells that can detect light. The number and density of these cells are very high in the middle of the retina (called the fovea), but if you go a little farther from its center, the number of these cells decreases. Only about six million of these cells (called cones) can detect colors, and less than one million of these cells can detect blue photons. It is said that more than 110 million cells (called rods) can only detect white light but cannot see colors. Only cones can work in daylight. Rods become saturated in so much light and do not work. So we can say that the resolution of the eye during the day is only 6 million or 6 megapixels but during the day the eye can see different colors very well. In low light the resolution of the eye increases but then it cannot see the color. That's why we can't see the color when the light is dimmed immediately.

But eye problems do not end there. Between the lens of the eye and the retina are the blood vessels and nerves that transmit the image formed on the retina to the brain in electrical waves. Think of them as eye wiring. As if the wiring of your eyes is a barrier between the lens of the eye and the retina of the eye and prevents the formation of a better image on the retina. In contrast, in modern camera sensors, the wiring is behind the sensor so that the beam rays can focus on the sensor. In the eyes of some animals, this wiring is behind sensors, including the octopus and its close relatives. That's why octopuses have very sharp eyes.

He boarded the train back from the same station And by chance he met Mr. Aqil again. He told his whole story to Aqil Sahib(respectful). Aqil Sahib laughed and said, "It is my good fortune that I will be your guide in this excellent journey."Let's go to the canteen, have some tea and start our journey.

Aqil: Look, you have to understand religions first. Son, religions are categorized as Semitic and non-Semitic and then non-Semitic religions as Aryan and non-Aryan religions.

The Semitic religions are the religions that were revealed to the Semitic people. According to the Bible, Shem(سام)is the name of Prophet Noah's son. Whose race is called Shemi(سامی).The Semitic religions, therefore, refer to the religions revealed to the Jews, Arabs, Assyrians, and Phoenicians (the ancient inhabitants of the southeastern shores of the Mediterranean who invented the alphabet), etc.

Let me tell you about non-Semitic religions.

Non-Semitic religions are further divided into two categories.

1. Aryan

2. Non-Aryan

Aryan religions refer to the religions that appeared in them. The Aryans are called the powerful tribes who spoke Indo-European languages and spread to different regions from Iran and Northern India from 2000 to 1500 BC.

Aryan religions are further subdivided into Vedic and non-Vedic religions.

1. The Vedic religion is called Hinduism or Brahmanism.

2. Non-Vedic includes Sikhism, Buddhism, and Jainism, almost all Aryan religions are non-prophetic, Zoroastrianism is an Aryan non-Vedic religion that has nothing to do with with with Hinduism and claims to be prophetic.

Now let me tell you about non-Aryan religions, They started in different areas. Confucianism and Taoism appeared in China, while Shintoism appeared in Japan. Many non-Aryan religions do not have the concept of God.

This is the definition of religion. Now I will explain to you what is the concept of God in Hinduism.

Saleema: Ammar, look at that deer, this will be our breakfast today. Go, Ammar, hunt, and bring.

Ammar looked at Saleema's face in surprise, wondering how I could hunt this deer with empty hands.

Ammar: How do I hunt it?

Saleema: So let me teach you how to hunt. Look at the two deer in front of you. One is in perfect condition and the other is slightly injured. Which of these is the easiest prey?

Ammar: the one who is injured is easy.

Saleema: so son understands this rule. The injured is not easy, nor the one who is in the right condition is easy, the injured is careful and the one who is in the right condition is smart and full of energy. But they also have weaknesses, which are love and pride.

Ammar: how?

Saleema: When you show love to an injured person, he will treat you as an ointment and when he treats you as an ointment, you can easily hunt him down. And the one who is in the right condition will want to fight in the pride of his physical strength, power, and intellect. Don't fight, just bend over and accept obedience, then he will consider you weak. You take advantage of the opportunity to trap it and hollow it, it will be very badly caught in the trap of its pride, then you can easily hunt it. But remember, these two things will not happen in a person at the same time, if he is injured then pride will disappear and pride never stands based on the wound.

Now they had hunted deer and made it their breakfast.

Saleema: You know those two deer were my characters.

Ammar surprisingly seeing at saleema's mouth.

He was now thinking that death was all around him. O life, your and my journey were just that.

But one thought gives him a hope that if they had to kill me, they would have killed me first, why they kept me alive, they must have kept some way, they are just testing me. Just as god tests man, surrounded him by difficulties, spreading darkness everywhere, God sees whether my servant hopes for light or not, Trusts me or not. He further thought, when I have to die, why don't I try to survive? why don't I fight till the end? How long will I resort to this excuse that if I did this it will happen, if I do that it would happen.No more if. "If" weakens decisions, confuses man.

Suddenly the voice comes From Speaker again."Young man, if you want, you can go. You will be set free. If you stop, a great and holy goal will be your destiny. But to stop, you have to pass this test."

As soon as he heard the name of the holy goal, Yasir remembered his questions and decided that he would die only after examining this holy goal.

When Khalid asked the question, everyone turned to Khalid.

Khalid, my name is Sajid, and now I will tell you briefly about our goal, our goal is human freedom From Customs and rituals, religion, and so on. But it is only possible when we liberate the whole society from religion and customs So that we can live a modern and better life, we can do whatever we want without any restrictions. So let's first understand what religion is.

The words religion, sharia, and tariqah mean "path".In Sanskrit, the word "Dharm" is derived from Dhar meaning "to keep".

The term Dharm refers to the path, justice, or good morals. It is derived from the Arabic word "ذ-ه-ب" (z-ha-b), which means to go (walk) or pass.

According to my personal opinion "Religion is a strong trap of human thought in which, after being trapped, human life either suffers hell or becomes heaven, and every human being in this world is either helly or heavenly." (Taimoor Ajmal).

Scholars have defined religion from their point of view. Here are some of the ones which I found to be interesting:

Religion is based on the belief that there is harmony between us and the universe. (Macte Gart)

Religion is the belief that the universe is meaningful (Welsis)

Religion is the name of a set of restrictions (Salomon Reinach).

Religion is the name of the effort that man makes to reconcile with his   loneliness (Whitehead)

Religion is the name given to the heart of the supernatural beings or forces that occupy human life according to the clergy (Fraser).

Religion is the name of perfect need and dependence. (Shliar Makhr)

Religion is the creation of the terror of ancient man (Lacris)

Religion is the metaphysics that came through experience (Spingler)

Religion is an attempt to connect the desires and aspirations of the human mind with external forces that do not care about it at all (Hartmann).

Religion is akin to psychological imbalance (Fried)

Religion is our sense of superiority over human destiny (Marley)

Religion seeks to reconcile ancient customs with rational and scientific thought and to provide a solid rationale basis for meaningless action (unknown)

Religion is opium for the people (Karl Marx)

Fear of invisible forces is a superstition in the individual and religion in the collective (Hobbes)

____

THE SCALE

The damage done by this wiring to the image on the retina is corrected by our brain during the processing of the vision, that is, to compensate for it. so that we never realize that this wiring is an obstacle in our sight. This wiring comes out of the back of the eye in a bundle and goes to the brain. To do this, we have a hole in the retina of the eye, through which this wiring exits the eye in the form of an optic nerve. Obviously, because of this hole, there is a place in our field of vision where our eyes do not work. This place is called a blind spot. Our brain cleverly fills this blind spot in such a way that we are unaware that there is no vision in one place in our field of vision. To do this, the brain uses signals from both eyes to fill this space.

Because the position of this blind spot in both eyes is different, the information received from the signal of one eye fills the blind spot of the other eye, so we do not even consciously realize this blind spot. But if you close your eyes and see a scene with just one eye, you can easily discover this blind spot.

As we mentioned earlier the overall resolution of the eye is very low but there is a central point in which the resolution is very high. This place is called Fovea. We never consciously realize that the resolution of the field of vision other than this center is very low. This is because the eye moves 70 to 110 times a second, called microtremors. In other words, the eye quickly scans any scene. The brain integrates the information that makes us consciously realize as if we were seeing everything in high resolution. In addition, the brain creates depth in the scene by integrating the signals coming from both eyes separately, which makes the scene appear more high resolution.

All this discussion concludes that the resolution of the human eye is more known due to brain processing than the eye. But the resolution of the eye and the camera cannot be directly compared.

The camera and the human eye can see things to a certain extent and a distance, They make things very easy. It is not possible to see God with the eyes and the instruments(camera etc) that are present in this world.

Hazrat Imam Jafar said: "The eyes can see only those things which have color and condition and Allah is the Creator of colors and condition".

So the most popular religion among the Aryan religions is Hinduism, and most of its beliefs are based on the Sacred Vedas, Upanishads, and Gita. Hinduism is generally considered to be a pluralistic(polytheistic) religion. Of course, many Hindus also confirm this notion by believing in multiple Gods, some Hindus believe in a system of three God while some Hindus believe in thirty-three crore (330 million) Gods Educated Hindus who are aware of their religious scriptures insist that a Hindu should believe in and worship only one God.

Now we review the religious books of Hinduism and understand the concept of god. Of all the Hindu religious books, the Bhagwat Gita is the most famous.

Let me recite an Ashlok(verse) of this:

(Translate)

"That God is not born, He is immortal and He is the owner of the whole universe"

[Bhagwat Gita, Chapter 10, verse 3]

Now look at what is written in the Upanishads:

"Ekam evaditiyam"

(Translation)

"He is only one without a second"

[Chandogya Upanishad, Chapter 6, Part II, Verse 1]

"Na casya kasuj janita na cadhipah"

(Translation)

"Of him there are neither parents nor lord"

[Svetasvatara Upanishad, Chapter 6, Verse 9, Part II]

"Na tasya pratima asti"

(Translation)

"There is no likeness of Him"

[Svetasvatara Upanishad Chapter 4:19]

"Na samdrse tisthati rupam asya, na caksusa pasyati kas canaiam. Hrda hrdistham manasa ya enam,evam vidur amrtas te bhavanti"

(Translation)

"There is no likeness of him whose name is great glory"

[The Principal Upanishad by S. Radhakrishnan page 736 & 737]

[Sacred Books of the East, Volume 15, the Upanishad part II page no 253]

Let me tell you about the Vedas. The Vedas are considered to be the most important in Hindu religious books. There are four main Vedas:

1. Rig Ved
2. Yajur Ved
3. Sam Ved
4. Atharva Ved

Now let's see what Yajur Ved tells us:

"Na tasya pratima asti"

(Translation)

"There is no image of him"

[Yajurved 32:3]

The same Ashlok(verse) further states:

(Translation)

"as He is unborn, He deserves our worship"

Another place in the Yajur Ved is listed:

(Translation)

"There is no image of Him whose glory verily is great. He sustains within Himself all luminous objects like the sun etc. May He not harm me, this is my prayer. As He is unborn, He deserves our worship"

[The Yajurveda by Devi Chand M.A. page 337]

(Translation)

"He is bodyless and pure"

[Yajurved 40:8]

(Translation)

"He hath attained unto the Bright, Bodiless, Woundless, Sinewless, the pure Which evil hath not pierced. Far-sighted, wise, encompassing, he self-existent hath prescribed aims, as propriety demands, unto the Everlasting Years".

[Yajurved 40:8]

[Yajurved samhita by Ralph I.H. Griffith page 538]

Now let's go to the Atharva Ved:

"Dev maha osi"

(Translation)

"God is verily great"

[Atharvaveda, Book 20, Chapter 58, Verse 3]

(Translation)

"Verily, Surya, thou art great, truly, aditya, thou art great. As thou art great indeed thy greatness is admire: yes, verily, great art thou, O God".

[Atharveda Samhiti vol 2 William Dmight Whintney page 910]

Let's go now to the Rig Ved.

"Na tasya pratima asti"

(Translation)

"There is no image of Him"

[Yajur Ved 32:3]

"Ma chidanyadvi shansata"

(Translation)

"O friends, do not worship anybody but Him, the Divine One".

[Rigveda Book 8:1:1]

[Rigveda Samhiti Vol IX, page 1 and 2 by swami Satyaprakash Sarasvati and Satyakam Vidhya Lankar]

(Translation)

"The wise Yogis concentrate their minds; and concentrate their thought as well in the Supreme Reality, which is Omnipresent, Great, and Omniscient. He alone, knowing their functions, assigns to the sense organs their respective tasks. Verily, great is the glory of the Divine Creator".

[Rigveda 5:81]

[Rigveda Samhiti Volume 6 Page 1802 and 1803 by Swami Satya Prakash Saraswati and Satyakam Vidhyalanka]

Now finally look at the Brahma Sutra of Hindu Vedanta[Vedanta is a mixture of Veda and Anta, that is, the extremity of Gyan(knowledge and wisdom). Vedanta used to refer to the Upanishads but now it is the system of philosophy which is based on the Upanishads.] What it says:

"Ekam Brahm, dvitiya naste neh na naste kinchan"

(Translation)

"There is only one God, not the second; not at all, not at all, not in the least bit".

Son, if you want to understand the concept of God in Hinduism, you have to study their religious books in depth.

Saleema: He first trapped me in my arrogance then I made a mistake again I showed my wounds, he hunted me again. But now no one can hunt me, Because the hunter himself knows that now hunting is impossible because after that the hunter has no trap left, the hunter knows that after hunting twice the prey becomes so dangerous, he can hunts the hunter. Son Ammar never falls into the mire of arrogance, but humbly moves away and says goodbye to the next one. But only when everything is connected with yourself. And never show your wounds to anyone. Everybody here is a hunter. Some do it for hunger, Some call it a hobby, some call it fake masculinity and power. Now you have come to my state of mind, now we will together go ahead on Journey.

Ammar: But ... (Then he thought something) Sure

Now he began to struggle to free himself, As soon as he loosened his hands a little, he felt a knife in his hand, he freed himself from the ropes with the help of the knife, And then he kicked and broke the chair he was sitting on. Now he had only one minute left. As soon as he took a piece of wood and walked towards the snakes wrapped in the window, he realized that they are fake snakes.

He had just come out of the Window when an officer met him with a smile on his face and said, "Congratulations."

The biggest advantage of religion to us is that it is different for each person or group, and because of this they have dissenting between them. If we use these dissenting to create a fight among them, there will never be a complete religious Power. Some wise people from these religious groups who want to find the truth, we can easily make them rebel. And when they become rebels, they become our strength. And these rebels, wearing religious veils, join all religious groups. They have no interest in the differences between these groups. Rather, they use it to prevent religious groups from uniting against us. The hatred of these religious people against this person strengthens his rebellion. We do nothing but look for such people and treat them with love and respect for their ideas, making them realize that Society is jealous of your wisdom and creativity. In simple terms, we use the human psyche.

THE PATH TO THE TRUE LOVE

He had come out to drink tea, he was satisfied with the existence of God, Suddenly he asked himself who am I?

Do I know myself

Do I understand myself?

Why am I confused with God?

What confused me?

Some human beings believe in God and some do not, what is the reason?

What is the matter?

Isn't this all a game of intellect? But both have intellect, who believe in God and also who do not believe in God.

This is strange majesty, I have to go into the depths of it, but from where to get into it?

This ocean of majesty is in me, I have to understand myself.

I don't have authority. Why do my decisions falter?

Why these wars in me, why am I not satisfied?

What is inside me?

I'm not one, but how?

I have different rulers inside me, sometimes there is war, sometimes peace, sometimes unrest, Why all this?

After all, why don't these rulers who live inside me unite with each other, why doesn't this war end?

My external existence is a slave to these internal rulers.

Which of these rulers is my enemy, who is my friend?

I have to know myself, I have to conquer myself, then I will find God.

O God, My intellect acknowledges your existence, but now also insists on seeking you.

He was now heading for the desert, he remembered a friend who might have answered his questions.

He had entered the desert after a day's journey. He did not know the address of his friend, but he had heard from someone that he was a very popular figure in the desert. He only knew his name.

He addressed a villager, "Brother, I want to meet Rajwan."

Villager: Everyone wants to meet him. There is a fort near where last time I saw him, you go there and see him. Maybe there you can find him.

Sikander: Thank you

Now Sikander enters the fort, the fort which was once famous for its splendor has now turned into a ruin. Suddenly Sikander hears a voice.

"So Sikander finally you came".

Now let me explain to you the concept of God in Sikhism, First, understand that Sikhism is the sixth largest religion in the world in terms of its number of followers.

Here is the sequence:

1. Christianity

2. Islam

3. Hinduism

4. Buddhism

5. Judaism

6. Sikhism

Sikhism is a non-Semitic, Aryan, non-Vedic religion As if it does not belong to the major religions of the world but it is a branch of Hinduism which was grafted by Baba Guru Nanak in the late fifteenth century. It originated in Pakistan and the region of northern and northwestern India called Punjab, meaning "land of five rivers". Guru Nanak was born in Kshatriya (warrior caste) Hindu Family but was very much influenced by Islam and Muslims.

The brief definition of Sikhism is that; The "Sikh" word Derived from the "Sisya" (this Sanskrit word is more appropriate for the Guru, its translation is "Cheela") which means disciple or follower, Sikhism is the religion of 10 Gurus, the first being Guru is Baba Guru Nanak and The tenth and last Guru is Gobind Singh. The holy book of the Sikh religion is Sri Guru Granth (Basically "Granth" is known as a knot, then came to be used for the book as well., when Hindus were unfamiliar with paper, They used to write on it and tie these leaves in a thread.) it is also called Adi Granth Sahib.

The Five–'K's

The five distinctive marks of the Sikhs, the first letter of which is "K". is obligatory on every Sikh to Keep the five 'K's which also serve as his identity.

1. **Kesh** – uncut hair, which all the Gurus kept.

2. **Kangha** – comb, used to keep the hair clean.

3. **Kada** – metal or steel bangle, for strength and selfrestrain

4. **Kirpan**- daggar, for self defense

5. **Kaccha** – special knee-length underwear or underrawler for agility.

Mool Mantra – Basic Beliefs of Sikhism:

Any Sikh can best praise God according to his religion concerning "Mul Mantra" (a collection of basic beliefs of the Sikh religion). Which is present at the beginning of Guru Granth Sahib.

It is mentioned in Sri Guru Sahib Volume 1 Japuji, the First verse:-

(Translation)

"There exists but one God, who is called the true the creator, free from fear and hate, immortal not begotten, self-existant, Great and compassionate".

Sikhism instructs its followers to be cautious and to practice monotheism. It believes in a supreme God who is, unmanifest and is called "Ek Omkara".

In the manifest form, he is called "Omkara" which has a few attributes such as:

Katar – The creator

Sahib – The Lord

Akal – The Eternal

Sattanama – The Holy name

Parvardigar – The Cherisher

Rahim – The Merciful

Karim – The Benevolent

He is also called 'Wahe Guru' which means the one true God.

The Sikh religion, being a strict monotheist religion, does not believe in Avataravada (the doctrine of incarnation) of God in the form of a human being or any other body to perform a great command. God never appears in incarnation. Sikhism is also strongly opposed to idolatry.

Guru Nanak was very much influenced by the words of Sant Kabir(Poet). Therefore, there are couplets of Saint Kabir in many chapters of Sri Guru Granth.

One of the famous couplets of Sant Kabir is:

" Dukh mein Sumirana sabh kerein sukh mein karein na koya

Jo sukh mein sumirana karein to dukh kaye hoye"

(Translation)

"Everyone remembers God during trouble but no one remembers Him during peace and happiness. The one who remembers God during peace and happiness why should he have trouble?"

Now let me tell you about Zoroastrianism (Zoroastrianism is also called Magianism, Fireism and Parsiism).

Zoroastrianism is an ancient Aryan religion that originated in Persia (Iran) 2500 years ago. However, the number of those who believe in it is relatively small. Less than 130,000 worldwide, but it is one of the oldest religions in the world. Zoroastrianism, also known as Parsiism, was founded by an Iranian prophet named Zoroaster. The holy books of the Zoroastrians are Dasatir and Avesta.

In Zoroastrianism, God is known as "Ahura Mazda". "Ahura" means "Lord and Master" and "Mazda" means wise, so "Ahura Mazda" means "God is All-Knowing and The wise God".

Ammar, maybe you have forgotten your beloved? You know why this happened because she was not your destination, she was just the way, Which you used to reach your destination and your destination is God. As soon as you came to me and you saw the clear possibilities of seeking God in the paths I told you, you forgot the old path. You forgot your beloved.

Son, do you know why the love of today's boys and girls has failed? Because sometimes their destination is the body, sometimes a partner just to get rid of their loneliness, sometimes wealth, sometimes something else. They use the path of love to achieve all these things. Now when they get their destination, who returns from the destination, towards the routes(ways). A human takes the path to another destination after one destination. But the love of the soul has no destination in this world, The soul is imprisoned in the body. So Son, whose destination is the soul is imprisoned in the path of love till death because as long as there is breath, the destination cannot be found. But every day he feels closer to the destination. Sometimes the destination of one is the soul and not of the other, and sometimes the destination of both is the soul and sometimes the destination of both is not the soul. Son, who picks the soul as the destination, his path is very beautiful, in this way he gets the most beautiful thing of this world which is internal peace. And he who does not make the soul his destination and still adopts the path of love, then he goes through the torments of the world, restlessness, anxiety, pain, anguish all become his destiny and from them, he is ruined. Making the soul a destination also causes anguish and pain if the other's destination is not the soul but that pain and anguish is for a very short time and it makes you rare.

The woman is the creature of God, it is not a crime to love a woman, the creature of God deserves love. But it is not right to make the love of the creature a condition of god's search. Son, when you love the Creator, you will automatically love the creatures. But remember, if you want to reach God by loving the creatures, then there are flaws in the creatures. The creatures also follow devilish paths, This will cause you to lose the sophistication of your love. Yes, the creature can show you the paths, as I am showing, I didn't keep a creature's love as a condition to seeking God. I did not make myself a watchman of God. God is free, god loves direct communication with his creatures.

Yasir: Congratulations on what?

The officer laughs at Yasir's question and says, "Congratulations on surviving and also on passing the exam successfully. My name is Omar. Let me explain to you the purpose of being here."

Omar takes Yasir to the meeting room, where everyone greets him. Now Omar is addressing everyone and says, you have all been gathered here from different institutions. Now, after a short training, you will become a soldier of this mission.

A man raises his hand and asks the question, Mr. Omar, what is our purpose(mission)?

Omar: Our mission is very simple. We maintain the existence of the state. You all fought only battles till today, but now you all are going to be a part of the War. Battles last for two or three days in which force is used, you clash with your opponent, either your opponent defeats you or you defeat your opponent, battles are part of the War. In short, just understand that war is a book and battle is only one page of this book. Some are on the economic page of this book, some on the battle page, some on the justice page, some on the peace page, some on the crime page, some on the ideological page, and some on the rights page. But these pages differ from each other because they do not consider themselves a book. But these are many pages of the same book. Because of their misunderstandings, the book which is War is constantly weakening. It is also a ploy of the enemy to make these pages unfamiliar with the book. The book is on the verge of destruction, and the day the book will destruct, the pages will fall apart. Then no matter how many battles are we won by our force, the enemy will destroy our economic page. Every page belongs to each other, so for a strong book, every page must accept that they relate to the book. It is important to win the war to protect the state and to fight it with the combined strength of all the pages.

But its biggest disadvantage is that if a society unites on it, it gets on the path of development, they become a very strong force, they are an ideology, which is not easy to stand against. It brings peace and prosperity.

Rituals and tradition are not very different from religion but they can be compromised, they are kept below the level of obligation but sometimes they are above the level of obligation. Rituals are very useful to us because religion can only be weakened through rituals. If we can able to arrest anyone in the pride of rituals, it would lead to nationalism or racism which will destroy religion. The root of nationalism is ritual and tradition and the root of ritual and tradition is ignorance of religion. Religion itself has many customs and traditions. Which has the status of obligatory. But when a man is caught up in desires, he makes his customs or introduces his tribe to a new custom, he takes it beyond the level of obligation. So that the rituals and customs become necessary and fixed and travel from generation to generation, And in later times when the wise person criticize, So someone should be present in defense of the rituals made by him.

But yes, these customs and traditions are also the beauty and identity of nations and also the guarantee of love between different nations. But only when they are not elevated to their level. Only adhere to those rituals and customs, which does not hurt the right of individuals, which is not against religion. Many Nations have one religion, but their customs are different. Therefore, the guarantee of peace is religion, not ritual. If the tradition and rituals are discounted, the religion will be strengthened. Religion unites many nations and these united nations give birth to a strong society. And these societies give birth to a state. A strong and peaceful state.

If people understand this, then it can cause detriment to us. Rituals and tradition should never be taken lightly.

LOVE & LUST, WEAKNESS OR POWER?

Sikander: Yes, I came, Rajwan, but did you wait for me? Do you know why I have come to you?

Rajwan: Yes I know why you have come to me, I know about everybody who comes to me.

Sikandar: But how?

Rajwan: Look, there is a law in this World namely the Law of Attraction, if I have answers to your questions then your questions pull you towards me and my answers pull your questions. And when my answers and your questions meet with each other, they will be completed, and we both will be comfortable. Just as questions bother a person, so do answers bother a person. So for the comfort of both of us, it is important that your questions found my answers and your eyes telling half of the story that what you want. I know you're here to find yourself, but it's not easy.

Sikandar: I know this, but I want to know myself.

Rajwan: For this, you will have to work hard, but I will make you aware of your enemies. So that you may succeed in your quest. Let's eat some food first. Then we will talk further.

They had now gone down to the castle, where there was a cold room. Rajwan shouted, "Bring food, the guests have come."A very beautiful and young girl entered the room with food and left the food. After the girl left, Sikandar asked Rajwan who this girl was.

Rajwan: She is a traveler like you, she doesn't say anything, she just listens to me, and she handles the cooking here.

After eating the meal, the same girl enters the room and rajwan tells her to show Sikandar, his room. Sikandar follows the girl, Sikandar had probably never seen such a beautiful girl before, all the way Sikandar was immersed in her imagination of beauty. Suddenly the girl stopped and pointed Sikandar to his room. As the girl started to leave, Sikandar asked her name. The girl turned around and looked at Sikandar with questioning eyes and then left.

Now, as soon as Sikandar got up the next day, he stood at the door and found Rajwan waiting for him.

Sikandar and Rajwan were now on the roof of the castle, which had become so weak that it could fall at any moment.

Rajwan addresses Sikandar and says, Listen Sikandar, Satan is evil, and the angel is good and you are Sikandar, the human, the union of good and evil. You are the nafs, Sikandar. ('nafs' is an Arabic word, literally means "self" and has been translated as 'psyche', 'ego' or 'soul') Your enemy is also your nafs and your friend is also your nafs, As long as you are unfamiliar with it, it is your enemy and when you are unfamiliar with it, it will become your friend. Until now this was the barrier between God and you, but if you understand the nafs, it will take you to God with this also you will found yourself.

––––––––––––––––––––

According to Dasatir, (Dasatir is the name of a collection of about 16 books compiled by the followers of Azar Kivan in the Safavid era. Azar Kiwan was one of the great scholars of Zoroastrianism who came to India with a group of his followers and founded a religious sect which is a combination of Zoroastrianism, Islam, Hinduism, and Christianity. The beliefs of the Azar Kiwan sect are recorded in the Dasatir.) Ahura Mazda has the following qualities:

1. He is One.

2. Nothing resembles him

3. He is without an origin or end.

4. He has no father or mother, wife or son.

5. Without a body or form.

6. Neither the eye can behold him, nor the power of thinking can conceive him.

7. He is above all that you can imagine of.

8. He is nearer to you than your own self.

Qualities of God according to Avesta:

According to the Avesta (religious book of the Zoroastrians), "Gathas" and "Yasna" describe some of the characteristics of Ahura Mazda such as:

1. **Creator**

(Yasna 31:7 & 11) (Yasna 44:7) (Yasna 50:11) (Yasna 51: 7)

2. **Most Mighty** - the greatest

(Yasna 33:11) (Yasna 45: 6)

3. Beneficent - '**Hudai**'.

(Yasna 33: 11) (Yasna 48: 3)

4. Bountiful - '**Spenta**'.

(Yasna 43:4,5,7,9,11,13,15) (Yasna 44:2) (Yasna 45:5) (Yasna 46:9) (Yasna 48:3)

Son, the Zoroastrian religious book consists of five parts.

1. **Yasna**

2. **Yashta**

3. **Vespard**

4. **Vendidad**

5. **Khordeh Avesta**

The religious anthem in Yasna is called Gatha. Some of which are Zoroastrian anthems.

Ammar, man learns from two things, one from observation and the other from knowledge, if a man starts learning from these things at the same time, he brings Action into existence. You can not get god only by thinking, you have to bring the action into existence, the power to act is in the body and in the thought of bringing the action into existence.

Come on, let me show you some places of worship today, they are near.

Yasir raised his hand to hear all this and addressed Omar and said "I have some questions, can I ask?"

Omar: Yes, you can ask.

Yasir: why should it fight behind/for the religion? I remembered God when I shot the bullet. Whom I shot he Also remembered God. But maybe God likes my religion that's why God has not saved him on his call or maybe we both were in the wrong religion, God was with someone else's religion. Therefore God leaves this decision based on "who has power will rule". But why doesn't God come forward (in front of the world) and sort out this matter or he likes this massacre? If a person of One religion dies at the hands of a person of another religion, his fellow religionists call him a martyr and non- religionists call him a hellish person. Either the dead of all religions are Martyrs or all of them are hellish or is human just doing all this in his stupidity or by using the name of God, the wise men using all humanity to achieve their goals for centuries. And its mind-building continues for a sacred religious purpose and who becomes a wise and raise question on this holy religious goal is killed, as they declared him infidel(kafir). Maybe this is the world of infidels. Here, a believer of one religion says infidel to the believer of another religion. And the believer of other religion says infidel to others religion person. Even the circle of infidels goes on and on like this world which is rotating in a circle.

Omar looks at Yasir's face carefully and says that Mr. Yasir has asked very important questions. I will answer all of his questions.

––––––––––––––––––––

Now Khalid came out after taking a class.

He was thinking deeply, what was he looking for here, and what was he being taught here? This world was completely new to him. He began to miss his friends, his family. He was just thinking that we all wanted to live peacefully, But when someone kills a person's family, how can he live in peace? Revenge becomes obligatory on him. But every time revenge is taken, why doesn't this fight end? Who is the real culprit? Who is on the truth? What is right?. Tears welled up in his eyes as he thought of this.

Suddenly he felt someone's hand on his shoulder. As soon as he turned around, he saw a member of his tribe standing in front of him.

He came to the tribe all of a sudden, and when everyone asked, the Sardar(hetman) only said that this is my relative, he had gone to the city to study since childhood, now he has returned to the service of the tribe as a young man.

Khalid: Talha, how are you here?

Talha: As you are here, I came here a few months ago. Don't cry my brother We have all lost someone. I am here at the behest of my good Sardar (hetman), And I know a lot, You are the only one I can trust. I see some questions in your eyes. Please be patient. I will answer all your questions. But after two days, now you have to go to your room. And yes, be careful, they will play with your mind and wipe out humanity, just keep your mind present. Now I have to go and do not tell anyone about what I have told you. Otherwise, we will both get into trouble.

Khalid now goes to his room. He attends class early in the morning. Sajid enters the room as usual and along with him some girls also enter the room. Khalid gestures to all the girls to go and sit with their companions. After that, Khalid addresses everyone:

"Today's lesson is very important for men and women. A human's greatest weakness is his emotions and these emotions are also his strength. The relationship that develops between a man and a woman has two names, one is love and the other is lust. Love is both, weakness and strength. But lust is the only weakness, the one who has it becomes its slave. But love is a pure relationship and a permanent place. Love is power for us, because if it is metaphorical love, then human is aware of the difference between right and wrong, there is obedience in it, it is beyond lies. If you fall in love with someone who is not on your purpose, you will not deviate from your purpose, but you will become weak. That person will not be able to change your ideology, but you will allow them to integrate their ideology with yours. And if someone falls in love with you then you know how to weaken their ideology. But love is a weakness for us because if it happens to God or what people call real, then the person who loves God, you feel him very easy and merciful to you. But inside he will be a storm, only a fool will fight with him. It is impossible to change his ideology(mind). We tried very hard to change the minds(ideology) of such people but maybe they already read our minds. They are not interested in money or anything else, it seems that they are living with all-knowing secrets. Well, now come to the lust. This is the greatest weakness of human nature But our strength because human is blinded by lust, and especially the man who has the lust for wealth(money) and woman is our favorite. I know this sounds bad to you, But sometimes bad things have to be used to get good things, Just like in wars, peace is achieved by shedding human blood And our goal is freedom, first of all from religion, then from all kinds of customs, and state slavery, we will free to do whatever we want.

From today, you men and women will be together and will try to overcome this passion of your love and lust.

THE CIRCLE OF INFIDELS

The nafs ('nafs' is an Arabic word, literally means "self" and has been translated as 'psyche', 'ego' or 'soul') is a combination of three things.

1. Body
2. The five senses
3. Mind

Understand the body first, the body is just a garment, it has two needs, food to live, and reproduction (sex) to never die. He only wants to satisfy his hunger and grow (increase the breed).

The five senses are following:

1. Sight (vision)
2. Sound (hearing)
3. Smell (olfaction)
4. Taste (gustation)
5. Touch (tactile perception)

These five senses collect information.

Now let's come to mind. This is the Central Processing Unit. The mind is an analyzer. In short, understand that the information that the senses collect, the mind produces output by processing them. The mind is an intelligence and security software whose job is to protect the body and fulfill its requirements. The five senses are Data collector Agents. Who gets the power supply from the body. All three are guarantors of each other's safety And completely useless without each other. The pleasure in sex is the fuel of the mind, and the organism transfer in sex is the fuel of the body. And yes, one thing to note is that the mind and the brain are separate from each other but interconnected. Just as the body can be touched but not the soul, so the brain can be touched but not the mind. The mind is thinking software. And the brain is made up of many cells. The brain is a hard drive where all the data is stored.

Son, Now I will tell you about the concept of God in the major Semitic religions.

Judaism is one of the most important Semitic religions. Its followers are called Jews and believe in the prophetic mission of Prophet Moses (peace be upon him).

In the fifth book (Deuteronomy) of the Bible, the following is the Hebrew command of Prophet Moses (peace be upon him) which tells us about God.

" Shama Israelu Adonai Ila Hayno Adna Ikhad"

It is a Hebrew quotation which means.

"Hear, O Isreal: The Lord our God is one Lord"

[The Bible, Duet 6:4]

Here are a few more verses.

"I, even I, am the Lord; and besides me, there is no saviour."

[The Bible, Isaiah 43:11]

"I am lord, and there is none else

There is no God besides me."

[The Bible, Isaiah 45:5]

"I am God, and there is none else; I am God, and there is none like me".

[The Bible, Isaiah 46:9]

"Thou Shalt have no other Gods before me. Thou shalt not make unto thee any graven image, or any likeness of anything that is in heaven above, or that is in the earth beneath,or that is in the water under the earth. Thou shalt not bow down thyself to them, nor see them: for I the lord thy God am a Jealous God..."

[The Bible, Exodus 20:3-5]

The same message is the book of Deuteronomy:

"Thou shalt have none other Gods before me. Thou shalt not make thee any graven image, or any likeness of anything that is in heaven above, or that in the earth beneath, or that is in the water beneath the earth. Thou shalt not bow down thyself unto them, nor serve them: for I the lord thy

God am a Jealous God..."

[The Bible, Duet 5:7-9]

Let's talk about Christianity, Christianity is a Semitic religion. which have about two billion followers in this world. Christianity is attributed to Jesus Christ (peace be on him).

Saleema takes Ammar towards these places of worship, There are places worship of three or four different religions together.

Saleema: Look at these places of worship, they belong to different religions, But there is only one cry of the people there and that is "God".There are people from different religions and they only believe in their God which is defined by their religion. They consider their way of worship to be the right thing to do and others wrong. See, this confusion is made by human beings, otherwise, you just think that why god wants his worship in different ways from some creatures and different from other creatures?

Ammar: So why is God listening to the cries of others who do not know God properly?

Saleema: Man-made a distinction in God (divided into many). But God is God, He does not discriminate between creatures. He gives to him who is heedless and He also gives to him who is aware. Now Saleema and Ammar were preparing for the return journey when Ammar suddenly saw his girlfriend who now came out of the synagogue with her husband. Ammar stopped, and the events of the past began to unfold before his eyes. Saleema suddenly noticed the stopped of Ammar and changing expression on his face that this is the girl whom Ammar loves. Suddenly Ammar wanted to take a step towards his love but Saleema stopped him.

Saleema: Stop, Ammar! what are you doing?

Omar: Look Yasir, every religion in the world teaches peace. All religions(followers) are happy in their areas. But every religion teaches preaching in which there is no evil, every human being is free to follow any religion he wants. But when one religion spreads too fast through preaching, other religions begin to weaken, and that is where the war begins. Let's try to understand this in simple language, consider that you are a Muslim, your religion is Islam, The society in which you live in an Islamic society, But you have another brother who lives in another corner of the world, He is also a Muslim but he does not live in an Islamic society. Now, if he spreads the teachings of Islam, people who agree with him will accept Islam, This is how the changes in this society will begin, Its system will begin to change. By the change of this system, if someone has a formal, religious, or power loss, he will try to stop the followers of this new religion(Islam). If they do not stop, he will oppress them. Will try to take away their ideological freedom. This is where the story begins. Every religion commands war against oppression and teaches peace. Now you, who are Muslims will take a step forward to help your distant Muslim brother. You will first explain(Peace and freedom message) to the oppressor, he will not understand, he will attack you. You will defend yourself and retaliate. Now that the weapons of the two religions have collided, the war has begun. Now the world has seen that the two religions have fought each other. Now Satan will never allow peace to prevail. And infidels(disbelief) is not an insult, infidels(disbelief) means denial of God's commands, And every religious believer thinks that the other religious believer is in denial of god's commands. Because of this, they consider non-believers(infidels) to be hellish. Hell is the place of the infidels, God's commandments are peace, justice, and nature. And why should God come forward and call a ceasefire?. These wars are fought for economic gain, power, peace, or justice. Is it God's work now to reconcile between you?. He has given you wisdom for this which you may have forgotten to use. Yes, God supports the truth. And the name of God is on the lips of those who kill and those who die because they think that I am the true soldier of God, the rest are disbelievers(infidels). And yes, the human intellect has used religious weakness for their benefit. But wars have been fought for truth and are still being fought.

I hope you understand everything which I said.

Now Khalid asks the girl her name who is sitting next to him.

My name is Nida and yours?

My name is Khalid.

Now Sajid's voice echoed in the hall that all the boys and girls should go to their respective rooms. After three days of training, all of you boys and girls will stay together.

Now Khalid was constantly thinking about this girl(Nida). He was given training in self-defense in the next two days. In which his companion was nida. He was now well acquainted with Nida. Now he was just waiting for the last day after which he had to be free from all restrictions. And he could stay with his favorite girl at any time.

Khalid was resting in his room at night when suddenly Talha entered his room through the window. Khalid asked in fear why did you come through the window?

Talha said, "We don't have time, hurry up. We have to get out of here. They have found out about us and also that I have told you secret things."

Khalid said, "No, I will not leave here. I doubt that you are on the wrong path. I don't even know you well."

Talha: I knew they would change your mind. Foolish boy, the girl named Nida, in whose love you are going mad, has warmed the beds of many boys like you in the name of love, and those boys have fallen into the trap of her love, destroyed everything, and are now lying in the grave.

Khalid: If it were all a trap, why would they tell so much about the psychology of love? Why did they explain their traps to me?

———————————————————————————

THE TEST

There is no gender of the nafs. It is common to both men and women. You cannot control the self(nafs) with the intellect. If you want to control the nafs and defeat it, you have to know about the nafs. Because the intellect is limited, no matter how much intellect you use, as soon as you solve a problem with your intellect, a thousand more problems will arise.

There are two characteristics of the self (nafs).

1. Active Self
2. Guilty Self

Active Self does the work, orders analyze and persuades to do any work, From the human body, good and bad deeds are taken by Active Self. When Active Self goes through what he has to do, then the movement of Guilty Self begins, it creates a contradiction, confusion. Every idea, every thought passes through these two Nafs(self), Active and Guilty. There is confusion and conflict even in the smallest work and thought. There is a choice hidden in this confusion and contradiction. As soon as any bad intention comes to your mind, the Guilty self will immediately start opposing it. And Active Self will be engaged in its persuasion.

Whichever of the two characters(Active Self and Guilty Self) dominates, the result will appear according to his will. And the loser in this decision-making role becomes immensely powerful and takes strong revenge once the result is out.

Christians insist on the divinity of Jesus(PBUH), but a study of the holy Christian books makes it clear that Jesus(PBUH) never claimed divinity. In fact, there is not a single unequivocal statement in the entire Bible where Jesus(PBUH) Himself said: "I am God" or where He says: "Worship Me." The Bible contains statements attributed to Jesus (PBUH) in which he preached quite the contrary. See the following statements attributed to Jesus Christ (PBUH):

"My father is Greater Than I"

[John 14:28]

"My father is Greater Than All"

[John 10:29]

"... I cast out Devils by the spirit of God..."

[Mathew 12:28]

"... with the finger of God cast out Devils...."

[Luke 11:20]

" I can mine own self do nothing: as I hear, I judge: and my Judgement is just: because I seek not my own will, but the will of the Father, which hath sent me."

[John 5:30]

"Think not that I am come to destroy the law, or the prophets: I am not come to destroy, but to fulfill. For verily I say unto you, Till heaven and earth pass, one jot or one title shall is no wise pass from the law, till all be fullfilled.

Whosoever therefore shall break one of these least commandments, and shall teach man so, he shall be called the least in the Kingdom of heaven: but whosoever shall do and teach them, the same shall be called great in the Kingdom of heaven."

[The Bible, Mathew 5:17-20]

"... and the word whic h ye hear is not mine, but the Father's which has sent me."

[The Bible, John 17:3]

"And this is life eternal, that they might know thee the only true God, and Jesus Christ, whom thou has sent."

[The Bible, John 17:3]

"Ye men of Israel, hear these words: Jesus of Nazareth, A man approved of God among you by miracles and wounders and signs, which God did by him in the midst of you, as ye yourself also know."

[The Bible, 2:22]

Ammar: I only want to talk to her once.

Saleema: Don't you see that she is with her husband? Do you want to destroy her married life? Do you want to make him suffer again? She did not betray you. She accepted all these things, after knowing that you were dead. You loved her soul or didn't you? Or did you determine the destination by using the path of love which was something other than the soul? Did you love her to find God? If so, stop and let her go. If not, go and demolish her married life And also kill the one who tried to kill you, Go and satisfy your ego. The decision is in your hands.

Ammar stops and sadly asks Saleema why this test is on me.

Let's move on to the next aspect. Let me tell you about the intelligence agency. Like all other countries, our country's intelligence also performs two basic functions.

First, it informs the state about the intentions of the enemy or potential enemy's movements and tactics, war preparations, etc.

Second, it enables the state to respond to timely nefarious acts by keeping track of the unwanted elements, regional and linguistic neural groups, enemy operatives, spies, and armed rebel groups seeking internal distraction. And we are part of that intelligence agency.

Let's understand some of the traps and ways of the enemy from which he attacks us.

1. Secret surveillance of countries' defense, external affairs, and technology departments, economic development, and educational programs and political institutions.

2. Subtle tactics like propaganda, disinformation, terrorism, psychological tactics, murder, blackmail, bribery, and intimidation.

Talha: Stupid boy, this was done only to win your trust. The hunter uses separate traps for the foolish and the wise. They think you are wise So they played with your intellect, and now they will fool you and kill you. And you will be killed in the joy of your wisdom. They will remove the fear of fire from your heart. And without their saying, you will jump into the fire of your own free will. But your bravery does not matter to the fire, if you jump into the fire, the nature of the fire is to burn everything, and then you will also burn. Don't forget your Goal. Come with me.

Unwillingly, Khalid walks with Talha, Talha gives Khalid a pistol and says, "use it on the enemy when needed and keep one bullet safe, shoot yourself before catching them or else you will be waiting for death, they will give you a lot of pain".Now as soon as they come out of the window of the room. They see Nida standing in front of them. Nida addresses Khalid, "Stop, Khalid, I don't know what you have to do with this man, but don't go, I have fallen in love with you. Either take me with you or stop for our love."

Before Nida could say anything more, Talha shot Nida in the head, suddenly the alarm went off. And Khalid put the pistol out on the head of talha.

Khalid: You killed my love in front of me, I will not leave you.

THE PATH TOWARDS THE GOD

After every crime has been committed under the influence of Action Self persuasion, the culprit's Guilty Self creates a strong feeling of guilt, Which we know and recognize as shame, blame, and regret. As the nafs are trained, a third character emerges which is called the teasing self. It has the ability to ridicule, laugh at yourself and look critically at your self-esteem. It does not take birth suddenly, but it is born in a very unusual way. It is born of the knowledge of the self(nafs). As the nafs become more trained, a fourth entity of the nafs emerges which is called Satisfied Self. It is self-satisfied, it does not cause anxiety. This is the nafs of the servant who finds God. This is the highest and most educated character of the self(nafs). Without finding God, more and more teasing Self can be created.

No one has complete and proper knowledge of Nafs(Self), but I am telling you that every emotion of yours is connected with your Nafs, every action of yours is connected with your Nafs.

That's enough for today. Let's take you to a garden now.

The garden in this deserted castle? Sikandar shockingly asked.

Rajwan: Yes, you just follow me.

Sikandar and Rajwan pass through a tunnel in the fort and ascend into an open field, Where there is a lot of green trees, and a waterfall of water is flowing from the hill. The Sikandar sees the same girl sitting there. Sikandar boldly asks Rajwan who this girl is?

Let me tell you about Islam. Islam is a Semitic religion. The number of his followers around the world is more than 1 billion 20 crores. If you want to understand the concept of God in Islam, you have to seek help from the Qur'an. A surah of the Qur'an called Surah Ikhlas, which is the one hundred and twelfth surah of the Qur'an, contains a very short but comprehensive definition of God. Which consists of only four verses.

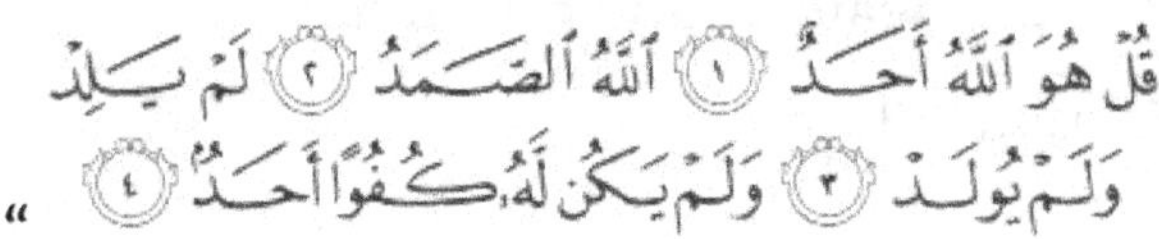

"

(Translation)

" 1. Say: He is Allah, The one and only.

2. Allah, the Eternal, Absolute.

3. He begets not, nor is He begotten.

4. And there is none like unto Him. "

[Holy Qur'an 112:1-4]

Let us now consider some more verses that tell us about God.

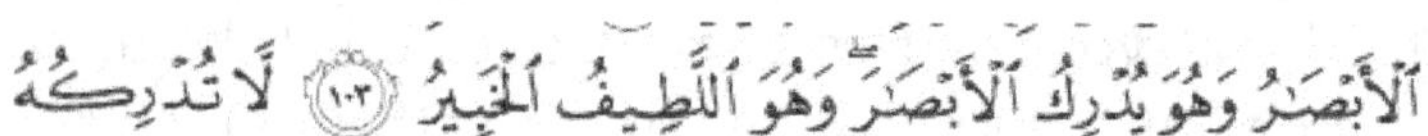

"   "

(Translation)

"No vision can grasp Him But His grasp is over All vision: He is Above all comprehension, Yet is acquainted with all things".

[Holy Qur'an 6:103]

"   „

(Translation)

"He is the great, the Most High".

[The Holy Qur'an 13:9]

"   „

(Translation)

"And He it is that Feeds but is not fed."

[Holy Qur'an 6:14]

"   "

(Translation)

"But He - the living, The self-subsisting, Eternal. No slumber can seize Him Nor Sleep. His are all things In the heavens and on earth."

[Holy Qur'an 2:255]

" لَيْسَ كَمِثْلِهِ شَيْءٌ "

(Translation)

"There is nothing whatever like create him".

[Al- Qur'an 42:11]

مِثْقَالَ ذَرَّةٍ إِنَّ ٱللَّهَ لَا يَظْلِمُ

"   "

(Translation)

"Allah is never unjust In the least degree".

[Holy Qur'an 4:40]

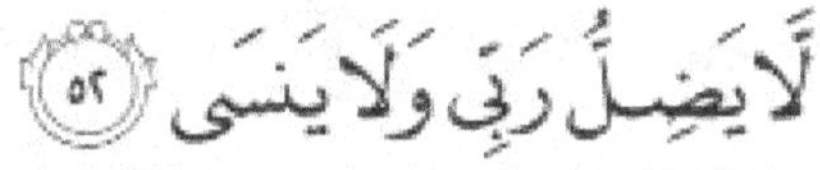

"   "

(Translation)

"..... my lord never errs, nor forgets".

[Holy Qur'an 20:52]

" أَنَّ ٱللَّهَ عَلَىٰ كُلِّ شَيْءٍ قَدِيرٌ "

(Translation)

"For verily Allah has power over all things."

[Holy Qur'an 2:106],[Holy Qur'an 2:109],[Holy Qur'an 2:284],[Holy Qur'an 3:29], [Holy Qur'an 16:77], [Holy Qur'an 35:1]

" فَعَّالٌ لِّمَا يُرِيدُ ١٦ "

(Translation)

"Allah is the doer of all the intends".

[Holy Qur'an 85:16]

عَمَّا يَصِفُونَ ٢٢ لَوْ كَانَ فِيهِمَا آلِهَةٌ إِلَّا ٱللَّهُ لَفَسَدَتَا فَسُبْحَانَ ٱللَّهِ رَبِّ ٱلْعَرْشِ

"   "

(Translation)

"If there were, in the heavens And the earth, other gods Besides Allah, there would have been

confusion in both! But glory to Allah, The Lord of the Throne:(High is He) above what they attribute to Him!"

[Holy Qur'an 21:22]

« مَا ٱتَّخَذَ ٱللَّهُ مِن وَلَدٍ »

بَعْضُهُمْ عَلَىٰ بَعْضٍ سُبْحَٰنَ ٱللَّهِ عَمَّا يَصِفُونَ ۝ وَمَا كَانَ مَعَهُۥ مِنْ إِلَٰهٍ إِذًا لَّذَهَبَ كُلُّ إِلَٰهٍ بِمَا خَلَقَ وَلَعَلَا

(Translation)

"No son did Allah beget, Nor is there any god Along with Him: (if there were many gods), behold, each god Would have taken away What he had created, And some would have Lorded it over others! Glory to Allah! (He is free) From the (sort of) things They attributed to Him!"

[Holy Qur'an 23:91]

Aqil: Look, son saad, I have tried to explain the concept of god in every religion in a very short and comprehensive way.

Saleema: Each destination has a test and each test has a price, The price for the exam is always paid, That price can be any sacrifice, patience, any difficulty. Then comes the test, And he who succeeds in the test finds the destination and he who fails is destroyed. You paid the price by that bullet which hits your chest and by lost your beloved. Now it's test time. If you succeed, you will find god, You will find your destination, The price you paid for this exam will become twice as a reward When you will achieve your destination. Look, these tests will make you stronger So that you can reach the destination. Without tests, your weak existence will break in half the way. Son the greatest enemy in the way of God is Satan, These tests will teach you to fight with Satan. If you do not escape the attack of the devil, you will lose everything. See how merciful God is. He has put an examination in his way, that if you succeed in the examination, you will be able to fight the devil, if not, you will not be able to take a step forward on this path. If you are forwarded without examination, you will be weak and the devil will take away everything from you.

Go, Ammar, Now the journey ahead will be yours without me.

Ammar: But you said that now I have only reached the level of you, the search for God is going on for you as well as for me, so our destination is one. How did these paths separate?

Saleema: Hahaha son Ammar I have reached the destination, I had both observation and knowledge. Everything I taught you was taught by observation. Now go back to your world and gain knowledge, find out what God is saying.

Ammar: But there are thousands of religions in the world, there are thousands of gods? How will I find out who is true?

Saleema: Searching on the principles of nature, you will reach God, Everyone will tell you that we have the true commandments of God, but remember, the commandments of God are not imaginary, God does not like fiction but reality. The commandments that seem true to you are true, but you have to go to the depths of the commandments. Because you will understand reality as reality only to the extent of your knowledge. Where your knowledge ends, reality will begin to seem imaginary to you. So, son, first increase your knowledge and then measure the reality.

---

3. Give any government such political advice that it is forced to adopt an enemy policy.

4. Providing financial assistance to minorities, student unions, and workers to support their agendas which is against the state.

5. To sponsor seminars, lectures, and film programs for scientists, intellectual scholars so that hostile thinking can be created in their minds against the state. To buy the loyalty of selected people(running state, influencers) by providing beautiful wives (which are the companions of the enemy) and wonderful jobs.

6. Providing bribes, honors, gifts, and assistance to some key politicians, journalists, government officials, and other key officials.

7. To provide advice and financial support to favorite political parties or politicians to run the political system of the state according to their intentions.

8. Violent demonstrations against the incumbent government to bring their political party to power and to provide full financial support to the so-called political movement to achieve this goal.

These are a few enemy tactics from which he achieves his goal.

Talha was a trained soldier, He immediately snatched the pistol from Khalid and said, "Foolish boy, if I want I can kill you easily. this girl wanted to go with us to spy on us. If you are not sure, search her."

When Khalid searches her, he finds a tracking device and a pistol in her clothes. Now Sajid realizes he was going to be deceived. He tells talha that you forgive me. I doubted you. Talha replied that it is not time to get emotional but to get out of here because the alarm is ringing. Now they both start trying to get out. Shootout starts now. Somehow Talha manages to get Khalid out of there. But Talha is injured by a bullet.

THE TRUE RELIGION

Rajwan: She is also a traveler like you and her name is Saleema. Let me tell you something more about the nafs.

Sikandar: Thanks Rajwan, but I know all these things. But despite knowing all these, I am not able to reach God.

Rajwan: Well, this is the problem. Let's say goodbye to Saleema first. Then I will try to solve this problem of yours as well. If you want, you can talk to Saleema. You can tell her about your journey and You can also learn about her travel.

After some time, Saleema and Sikandar talk to each other and come to Rajwan.

Rajwan: Goodbye Saleema, now you have to make your journey from here. Sikandar, come with me.

Look, Sikandar, your heart wants something else, your eyes want something else, your ears want something else, just as every part of your body wants different things according to itself. But your thinking wants god, you must first subdue every part of your body with your thinking. But you have to do it very wisely. Take the example that you have to stop a moving train or remove it from the track. If you come in front of it and stop it, you will suffer and the train will suffer too. Because you both have equal power. Let's adopt another method. Now you will drail the train from the side and remove it from the track. So it will not harm you, but when the train is removed from the track, it will be damaged. But if you stay safe, you will turn that loss into profit. Because the train is a lifeless thing, devoid of intellect. But you are a living thing and you also have intellect, you can recover this loss.

You have to find god with all your heart and mind and with all your passion. When your desire and your existence will demand the same thing, Then the power will be created in your demand, Which will be the power of craving, Which will lead you straight to God. But it will all happen when you know God's commandments. Go, Sikandar, you have to meet another person now. Whose name is Saad, he will acquaint you with the commands of God. And remember, if your longings and desires are true, you will find the Lord of the universe. And he who has found God has also found everything created by him. Go, Sikandar, may God protect you.

Now Sikandar had embarked on his new journey in search of Saad.

Saad: But I have found the followers of these religions opposite to their religious books, why this?

Aqil: We find the answer to your question from these religious books.

Allah says in Qur'an:

" صُمٌّ ۝ لَا يَرْجِعُونَ فَهُمْ عُمْىٌ بُكْمٌ "

(Translation)

"Deaf, dumb, and blind, They will not return (to the path)".

[Holy Qur'an 2:18]

The Bible gives a similar message in the Gospel of Mathew:

"Seeing they see not, and hearing they hear not, neither do they understand."

[Matthew 13:13]

A similar message is also given in the Hindu Scriptures in the Rigveda:

(Translation)

"There maybe someone who sees the words and yet indeed do not see them; may be another one who hears these words but indeed does not hear them".

[Rigveda 10:71:4]

See, son, all the great religions who believe in the existence of god are convinced of the existence of one god at the highest level.

As time went on, people often distorted religious books and scriptures with their own hands for their benefit. Due to which the scriptures were altered.The creed of many religions distorted From monotheism to polytheism or pantheism.

Saad: I understand your point, but which religion should I follow because every religion believes in one God. And this was the matter of the scriptures, can God be proved by intellect?

Aqil: See, all religions are pointing to the oneness of God, and the religious books of all the major religions are bearing witness to one God. Now, if you want to know which religion is the truth, then you have to check the rules of this religion such as social, justice, life. As I told you, many religions are no longer in their original form, so you have to find a religion of God that has only God's commands and no human intellect. For this, you have to measure all the rules of that religion on the scale of nature which you consider right. Every commandment of the true religion will bring progress, prosperity, and peace. In which man will get equal rights, which will teach justice. And the testimony of whose commandments will be giving every particle of this universe.

Look, son, your journey and mine were just that. Now you have to meet another person whose name is Sikandar Which will convince you of the existence of God with rational arguments. And will also enlighten you with yourself.

Now the train had reached its last station. Aqil and Saad said goodbye to each other. And now Saad was on his way to his new destination. Whose guider will be Sikandar.

Look, every holy preacher person looks like a friend of God but the reality is not like that. When you announce that you have set out in search of God, all the wolves will turn to you. Because they are always looking for a man who seeks God. They will ruin your life. A lot of artists have decorated their shop to sell god. Only you can survive from them all when you know, Otherwise, you will become their victims. Just think for yourself these big religious gatherings, grand urs, scholastic emotional speeches, did they find god from all of this? In reality, man wants to escape, and he gets the temporary benefit of joining them all, but he is still not satisfied because all these things give only a temporary benefit, the constant benefit which is God is still not found.

Go, Ammar, if life lasts, then we will meet again. Now the journey is yours and the destination is also yours.

Ammar: But what will you do here, come with me, far away from these mountains, thousands of people are waiting for you in my world, don't waste yourself, you are also God's creation and you are wronging yourself. Will God not take account of the injustice done to His creatures? Will you find God in these mountains? Do you know God's commandments? Come with me I know someone who will help us move forward and understand God better.

Saleema: What is the name of that person?

Ammar: That person's name is Saad. And he will make us aware of God's commandments. And will explain the concept of God in all religions.

Now Saleema and Ammar are embarking on their new journey.

There is only one purpose to gather you all here, The growing casteism in the country is poised to become a new state within the state, The enemy is using our brothers according to his tricks. All you do is make peace with angry groups, and find the enemy to reach its end. But remember that you are going to find enemies in them. In the same way, they have their supporters in us. The enemy will be identified as a traitor to the state and a conflict of common interest. Maybe we have enemies' spies between us. The enemy has reached the highest levels of our country. In every institution there are two kinds of people, one who is loyal to the country and the other who is a traitor and an ally of the enemy, They are creating differences between the people and the institutions. Hatred for the institutions is being instilled in the hearts of the people. The enemy wants to weaken the institutions so much that when they attack directly, the institutions cannot defend the country. He is making the people rebellious, and showing them dreams of a separate state based on casteism. He first wants to eliminate the central power of the state, which is collectivism. When collectivism is eliminated, it will be much easier for it to be eliminated separately. All of you go and make peace with your angry brothers and eradicate the enemy. You have to find your way and your purpose. You will see the disease of casteism everywhere in this country.

Now all of them get up and go out. Yasir also gets up with them and goes out. All of them take their belongings and start their preparations.

Yasir also starts preparing to move towards his journey. That suddenly Omar comes to him and says, "Yasir a journey is already waiting for you, you have to meet the leader of a tribe and you will tell him your name talha". And Omar goes after explaining the details.

Now Yasir is on his way, his body and soul remain the same but he gets a new name, "Talha".

Talha: Khalid, I don't have time now. Listen to me carefully. I am a soldier of this country, and I am part of an organization that is the guarantor of the ideology of this country and the protection of its peace. Your chief(Sardar/hitman) and I have been trying to end this war which is continued for years. And these are our real enemies. I get their many secrets. All you have to do now is just to reach the place which I'm telling you, with their location and USB which I'm giving you. And my name is Yasir, not Talha. I told you that I would answer your questions. You can ask me your questions.

Khalid: On one hand, God said the fight for your right, and on other hands, if we fight for our right. They declare us Rebel and then kill us using your (God) religion references. why is that?

Yasir(Talha): The differences are in every religion, they are in every institution, sometimes an institution emerges as a wrongdoer, sometimes the oppression of the whole state begins to fall on only one group. This is because some of the people in this group sell their faith and buy treason, the same thing happens in institutions. But this does not mean that the whole institution or the whole group is a traitor. But the enemy takes advantage of this, he presents the lie as reality, the traitors of this group are presented as oppressed in front of all the people, which makes the people against the state and state institutions, But when there is no way left the State to have to be taken Strict measures, and when war breaks out, the house of every person living in this town burns down, whether he is oppressed or a tyrant.

The group that is oppressed should go to the same state institutions after getting the education and go to the bottom of the enemy and those traitors who are present in the institutions and destroy their existence.

One thing to remember is that if someone in your household raises their hand against you, the rest of the family will not be against you. Rather, the battle will be settled first and then the decision of the elders will lead to peace. But if the same fight is fought with an outsider, then the people of your house(your family) will immediately attack the opponent, as long as the reconciliation reaches, there will be a lot of damage.

This example is of state institutions and groups. The attack on the person of a state institution is considered to be an attack on the whole institution. And the attack on one group's person is considered to be an attack on the whole group. Even if they both are wrongdoers and criminals.

So the best solution is not to come against each other to make decisions of justice or injustice. Rather, peace will be achieved only by mixing, institutions in groups and groups in institutions. The state in the people and the people in the state.

My blood has flowed a lot. It is very difficult for me to survive. You go, this USB should reach that place which I told you. You need more training. You are young and you are the guarantor of progress and peace. Now go, Goodbye.

After saying these last words, Yasir died. Now Khalid is embarking on their new journey with his new vision and Goal.

(The End)

THANK YOU

Thank you so much for choosing and purchasing my book on a topic with countless other options. I'm truly grateful that you selected my work. Your support means the world to me, and I hope you enjoyed reading it from start to finish.

I believe I've fulfilled my responsibility to share this information with the world, and now I'm turning to you. Your review can significantly impact independent authors like me. By sharing your thoughts, you'll help me continue creating books that provide valuable insights and solutions.

I'm curious to know what you learned and how the book impacted you. Your feedback will help me improve future works.

Click here to leave a review!

https://taimoorajmalawan1.blogspot.com/2021/10/me-and-goddownload-in-book-form.html

Feel free to connect with us, and to share your opinions, we'll be happy to hear you.

Click here to connect with us.

https://linktr.ee/taimoorajmalawan1

ABOUT THE AUTHOR

Taimoor Ajmal Awan

Taimoor Ajmal is a versatile Pakistani with a keen interest in law, technology, and personal growth. Hailing from Pakistan, his diverse educational background, encompassing both legal and technological fields, has equipped him with a unique perspective. With a passion for continuous learning, Taimoor has pursued numerous certifications and training programs, enhancing his knowledge and skill set.

Beyond his academic pursuits, Taimoor has explored his creative side as a published poet and author. His book, "Me and God," is a testament to his philosophical and spiritual inclinations.

A dedicated individual, Taimoor has also made significant contributions to his community through his involvement in various organizations and initiatives. His leadership qualities and commitment to personal development are evident in his accomplishments.

With a strong foundation in both theoretical knowledge and practical experience, Taimoor is poised to make a positive impact in his chosen fields.